THE LOUISIANA PURCHASE

A View of New Orleans in December 1803

(Courtesy The Historic New Orleans Collection, Museum/Research Center. Acc. No. 1958 42)

Louisiana Life Series, No. 7

THE LOUISIANA PURCHASE

by
Carl J. Richard

Published by
The Center for Louisiana Studies
University of Southwestern Louisiana
Lafayette, Louisiana

Cover image courtesy of the Louisiana Historical Society,
from the collection of the Louisiana State Museum.

Library of Congress Catalog Number: 94-74141
ISBN Number: 0-940984-91-1

Published by The Center for Louisiana Studies
P.O. Box 40831
University of Southwestern Louisiana
Lafayette, LA   70504-0831

The Louisiana Purchase

While the Louisiana Purchase was partly a product of fortunate circumstances, it was largely a result of the conscious and concerted policy of territorial expansion which Anglo-American leaders had pursued from the arrival of the first English settlers on the North American continent. Heirs to a European imperial tradition, Americans desired territorial expansion to achieve prosperity and power, to ease population pressures, to secure their borders against expansionist European monarchies, and to spread their way of life, which they regarded as inherently superior to the lifestyles of Native Americans and other European colonists.

The Louisiana Purchase was born of desire, fear, and a sense of mission, the same emotions which later produced the Mexican War and extended the United States' western frontier to the Pacific Ocean. Thomas Jefferson and other Republicans sought territorial expansion as a means of preserving the agricultural character of the United States. This desire was accompanied by the widespread fear that Napoleonic France's control of the mouth of the Mississippi River posed a grave threat to the future unity and security of the United States. Americans' continuous quest for secure borders resembled that of the early Romans, who also engaged in what historians have termed "defensive imperialism." Americans also feared that overpopulation would devastate their standard of living if the United States did not acquire new territory. During the eighteenth century the American population doubled every twenty years. Finally, many Americans believed that territorial expansion was the most effective means by which the United States could carry out its self-proclaimed mission to spread republicanism.

The French Colonial Background of Louisiana

In 1682 René-Robert Cavalier de La Salle became the first European to travel the length of the Mississippi River. La Salle named the vast lands watered by the river "Louisiana," after Louis XIV. Louisiana's French governors experienced great difficulty attracting and retaining good settlers. Louisiana could produce only inferior varieties of tobacco and indigo, and the protectionist Spanish colonies to the east (Florida) and west (Mexico) refused all but a little illicit trade with the French colony. Mortality rates on the voyages to Louisiana were as high as those suffered by African slaves transported to the West Indies during the same period. Once landed, large numbers of settlers died of scurvy, dysentery, malaria, smallpox, yellow fever, and other diseases. Louisiana remained a disappointment and a drain on French resources throughout the colonial period. As late as 1762 the colony possessed only three small centers of population and trade: New Orleans, Natchez, and Kaskaskia (Illinois). At that time Louisiana's population consisted of only 5,000 whites and 3,000 African slaves. Nearly half of the colony's inhabitants had been carried there against their will.

The French and Indian War (1754-1763) represented the final blow to French control over the underpopulated colony. Throughout the eighteenth century Great Britain and France, the two superpowers of the age, engaged in a series of colonial wars which culminated in the French and Indian War. When followed by victories in Pennsylvania, India, Cuba, and the Philippines, the British capture of Quebec (1759), the capital of New France (Canada), changed the map of the New World. In 1762, under the Treaty of Fontainebleau (subsequently ratified by the Treaty of Paris of 1763), France relinquished the western portion of Louisiana (the land west of the Mississippi River and the Isle of Orleans) to her Spanish ally in an effort to prevent its capture by the British. The French no longer needed the colony, which was costing France $1.75 million per year, to protect the southern approaches to New France. The Spanish did not really want Louisiana, but recognized its utility as a buffer zone between the populous and expansionistic Anglo-American colonies and the valuable colony of New Spain (Mexico) and dreaded its capture by the British. The following year, in the Treaty of Paris, the French were compelled to surrender to the British both New France and their claims to the eastern Mississippi valley. Thenceforth, the name "Louisiana" applied only to the western Mississippi valley. Within a single year the vast French empire on the North American continent had been completely dissolved. Under the treaty Spain was also forced to cede Florida to Britain in exchange for the return of Cuba and the Philippines, both of which had been captured by the British during the war.

The removal of their most powerful adversary from the continent filled Anglo-American hearts with pride and opened the Ohio valley to their settlement. But it also dramatically diminished American dependence on British military defense. In the place of powerful France only weak Spain and a small number of ill-equipped Native American tribes remained to block American expansion. American colonists no longer felt the need for British protection—at the very moment when Parliament began insisting that the colonists pay for it. In this way the French and Indian War helped produce the American Revolution.

Early American Expansionism

Even as early as the colonial period, Anglo-Americans had been infused with the belief that they were destined to create a Protestant empire in the New World. English colonies like Virginia claimed all of the land westward to the Pacific Ocean long after they discovered that the western coast was not just a few weeks journey away. American colonists often ignored Native American claims to the land, reasoning that God had predestined it for good Christians like themselves. The French and Indian War began when twenty-one year old Major George Washington demanded that the French vacate disputed territory in the Ohio River valley. Like numerous other American colonists, Washington had a personal interest in the outcome of the struggle. His brothers owned stock in the Ohio Company, which had purchased 500,000 acres of the disputed land from the British government. These land speculators hoped to reap a fortune by reselling the land to Anglo-American settlers in small parcels at a higher price. British King George III's Proclamation of 1763 infuriated them by prohibiting white settlement west of the Appalachian Mountains. Although the king's intent was to repair relations with Native American tribes, disgruntled Americans suspected the British government of attempting to limit the colonists' wealth and power by restricting their expansion. The proclamation was another leading cause of the American Revolution.

Washington was not the only American leader who supported territorial expansion during the late colonial period. In 1751 Benjamin Franklin praised "the Prince that acquires new territory if he finds it vacant, or removes the Natives to give his own People room." Four years later John Adams contended that though America had begun as a few scattered settlements, like the crude villages of early Rome, America would become "the greatest seat of Empire." The idea that "empire" always moved westward (as, in the past, from the Middle East to Greece to Rome to France to Great Britain) had long been a popular European belief.

American leaders continued to support expansion during the Revolutionary War. In 1775 the Continental Congress authorized Benedict Arnold's ill-fated invasion of British Canada. In 1777 Virginia financed George Rogers Clark's expedition to capture Fort Sackville in Vincennes, Indiana, a victory which laid the basis for American claims to the Ohio River Valley in the Treaty of Paris of 1783. In that treaty, which concluded the Revolutionary War, Great Britain recognized American independence and agreed to extensive boundaries for the new nation: the Great Lakes in the north, Spanish Florida in the south, the Atlantic Ocean in the east, and the Mississippi River in the west. The American commissioners at Paris, John Adams, Benjamin Franklin, and John Jay, almost succeeded in persuading the British to include the Canadian province of Ontario within the United States' borders. (Meanwhile, Spanish governor of Louisiana Bernardo de Gálvez's conquest of West Florida led to Britain's retrocession of all of Florida to Spain. The British loss of Florida and their thirteen American colonies caused them to turn their primary imperialist focus away from North America, thereby paving the way for future American expansion.) Struck by the vigor with which the Americans pressed their territorial claims, a British observer prophesied regarding the United States: "The pride of empire will awaken and conquests will be multiplied on neighboring borders. Florida and the Spanish possessions on the banks of the Mississippi will fall before them; and as they increase in power, that power will reach the limits of the Southern Ocean, and dispossess the Europeans of every hold upon the great continent of America."

American leaders issued similar prophesies. In 1785 John Adams predicted that the United States was "destined beyond a doubt to be the greatest power on earth, and that within the life of a man." Patrick Henry declared: "Some way or the other we must be a great and mighty empire."

The desire to create what Thomas Jefferson called an "empire for liberty" was perhaps best expressed by Thomas Paine in *Common Sense*, the pamphlet which convinced many Americans to support independence in 1776. Paine eloquently set forth a new mission for America, the secular and political counterpart of the Puritans' old religious mission of constructing a "city on a hill." The new American mission was to spread republicanism. Paine cried: "Freedom hath been hunted round the globe. Asia and Africa hath long expelled her. Europe regards her as a stranger, and England hath given her warning to depart. O, rescue the fugitive and prepare in time an asylum for mankind." (By asylum," Paine meant a refuge, not a sanitarium, contrary to the claims of some modern skeptics of American society.) The future happiness of the world depended on the spread of republicanism, and American territorial expansion was one of the most effective and agreeable means of spreading that ideology. But, though revolutionary Americans secularized the Puritan mission, converting it from a religious to a political quest, by no means did they rob it of all religious significance. Most believed that God had chosen the United States as His principal instrument for expanding republican government, a political system clearly superior to all others.

Federalists Versus Republicans

In 1788 all but two of the states ratified a new federal constitution for the United States. (North Carolina and Rhode Island would ratify shortly thereafter.) Based on a deep fear of centralized power rooted in British Whig ideology and powerfully reinforced by the recent "British tyranny," the United States' first federal constitution, the Articles of Confederation, had established a weak central government. In fact, under the Articles, the United States was not really a single nation, but a loose confederacy of thirteen separate nations (hence the very term "state," which implies a sovereign nation). But during the 1780s the actions of various states alarmed many Americans. Under pressure from unruly mobs, state legislatures began printing large sums of money to alleviate the plight of debtors (most of the population) through inflation. Rhode Island printed so much money that many creditors fled the state to avoid being repaid with the worthless currency. Creditors cried out for a strong federal government which would possess the exclusive authority to coin money. Enraged by the chaotic and potentially dangerous system of state tariffs on the goods of other states, merchants fervently supported the establishment of a federal government which would have the sole power to regulate trade. Land speculators and frontiersmen wanted a strong federal government whose ability to defend the frontiers against Native American tribes would increase the value of western land. Finally, James Madison, the "Father of the Constitution" himself, and many others felt humiliated by the inability of the United States' weak central government to command either national or international respect. The supporters of the Constitution feared interstate warfare, which might invite foreign intervention and domination, if order were not established soon. Maryland and Virginia were almost at open war over borders.

The U.S. Constitution of 1787 alleviated many of these problems. Congress was not only granted the exclusive power to coin money and to regulate commerce, but was also allowed to levy direct taxes and to maintain an army and navy in time of peace. (Under the Articles of Confederation, Congress could only request money from the states. It has been estimated that Congress received only about one-quarter of the funds it requested.) The new federal government was also designed to be immune from the "majority tyranny" which had led to the inflation of state currencies. Under the new Constitution, the House of Representatives was the only branch of government which would be directly elected by the people. (The president would be selected by an Electoral College whose members were not originally chosen by popular vote, senators would be selected by the state legislatures, and federal judges would be appointed by the president.)

Americans understood that a stronger central government would facilitate the nation's territorial expansion, a project most embraced with a sort of missionary zeal. In the famous *Federalist* No. 10 essay Madison defended the Constitution against Montesquieu's argument that republics must remain small if they wished to remain republics. The Antifederalist adherents of Montesquieu claimed that the United States must remain thirteen separate republics, uniting only for a few necessary purposes. Madison retorted that the number of factions in a large, commercial republic like the United States would be so great that majorities must be weak coalitions, incapable of prolonged tyranny. (Representation would enhance this effect by preventing majorities from acting on sudden impulse.) Hence, in the modern world, the truth was exactly the reverse of what Montesquieu had alleged. The larger the republic the greater its degree of stability and justice. Madison had provided a persuasive rationale not only for the Constitution itself, but for the expansionism that produced both the Louisiana Purchase and the Mexican War. If a republic which extended to the Mississippi River would be more stable and just than thirteen smaller republics, would not a republic extending to the Pacific Ocean be even more preferable?

George Washington, the first president under the new Constitution, considered national unity imperative. He balanced his cabinet evenly between nationalists and supporters of state rights. But, despite Washington's strenuous efforts, party sentiment soon arose as the result of Secretary of the Treasury Alexander Hamilton's fiscal program. Born out of wedlock on the island of Nevis, one of the Virgin Islands, Hamilton had been orphaned by age thirteen. The poor, but bright, boy had so impressed his employer, the wealthy merchant Nicholas Cruger, that Cruger had sent Hamilton to King's College (now Columbia University) for a thorough education. But Hamilton's education had been cut short by the Revolutionary War. Hamilton had served as Washington's chief aide during the war, had married the wealthy Philip Schuyler's daughter, and had then become a lawyer, a member of the Continental Congress, one of the leading defenders of the new Constitution, and the nation's first Secretary of the Treasury. He proposed the federal government's assumption of state debts and the payment of those debts at face value, an excise tax on whiskey, a national bank, and a series of measures to protect infant American industries from European competition, including subsidies, federally-funded internal improvements (roads and canals), and tariffs. Hamilton succeeded in securing congressional approval of all but the last proposal. A superior administrator, the energetic Hamilton created an efficient Treasury Department, established the public credit at home and abroad, and strengthened the currency, thereby helping to restore prosperity to a war-torn nation. As Daniel Webster later put it: "He smote the rock of the national resources, and abundant streams of revenue gushed forth. He touched the dead corpse of public credit, and it sprang upon its feet."

But Hamilton's fiscal program was divisive, dividing Congress into two distinct voting blocs. One group began calling themselves "Federalists," the other "Republicans." Concentrated largely in the relatively urban and commercial northeast, the Federalists feared both the dismemberment of the nation and majority tyranny. Concentrated largely in the rural and agricultural South and West, Republicans tended to be planters and small farmers. They feared federal tyranny, a presidential monarchy, and a commercial and financial oligarchy. Worshipers of the agricultural life, Republicans were horrified by Hamilton's program to "Europeanize" America—that is, to fill her cities with mobs of factory workers, whose depraved urban lifestyle and whose dependence on their employers would render them unfit for citizenship in a republic. Better to have a society of sturdy, independent farmers, whose land, by giving them a stake in society, would make them the backbone of the republic. The cabinet disputes between Hamilton and Jefferson soon erupted into a press war between the Federalist John Fenno's *Gazette of the United States* (New York, 1789) and the Republican Philip Freneau's *National Gazette* (Philadelphia, 1791). (Both editors received patronage from the leading politicians on each side. Fenno held government printing contracts, and Jefferson employed Freneau as a State Department translator.)

Lacking the modern concept of political parties as a positive good, each party suspected the other of treason. The concept of legitimate opposition did not yet exist. The equation of virtue with independence of thought and action, when combined with a concomitant equation of vice with "factionalism," contributed greatly to the antiparty sentiment which dominated the early history of the United States. According to the classical doctrine, membership in a political party inevitably involved defending the indefensible vices of one's allies and attempting to dominate one's fellow citizens in order to satisfy a narrow self-interest. In the eighteenth century the greatest compliment one man could pay another was to call him "disinterested." To be disinterested was to place justice above all other considerations, including one's own interest and those of one's family, friends, and political allies. Both Federalist and Republican leaders decried "party spirit." They considered their own parties temporary aberrations, necessary only to block the antirepublican ambitions of their opponents, and looked forward to the day when they could be safely eliminated. Nevertheless, even while decrying parties in the abstract, political leaders on both sides were engaged in organizing them.

It was the French Revolution which transformed mere party sentiment into organized political parties. The revolution had begun in 1789, only a few months into Washington's first term. A conservative and largely peaceful rebellion of the nobility against King Louis XVI, the revolution was almost universally applauded by Americans, who were gratified that the French seemed to be emulating them. But by 1793, the start of Washington's second term, the revolution had turned radical and bloody. Seeking to free himself from the constitutional restraints recently imposed upon him, Louis XVI attempted to flee France in order to rally foreign reactionary armies to restore him to absolute power. The ultimate result of Louis' foolish action was the triumph of the radicals, who tried him (as "Citizen Capet") and guillotined him. The radicals followed the execution with a reign of terror against all opposition, including the clergy and other radicals. Great

Britain joined a coalition of European monarchies which waged war against the French republic.

Despite his best efforts, Washington found it impossible to maintain a foreign policy which would satisfy both Britain and France, both Federalists and Republicans. Washington was anxious to avoid war with Britain, though the British had violated the Treaty of Paris of 1783 by refusing to evacuate their forts in the Ohio valley and though they were engaged in the seizure of approximately 300 American ships trading with France. (Washington understood that the United States had also violated the Treaty of Paris by seizing more loyalist property and by preventing Americans from paying their pre-Revolutionary debts to British merchants.) Aware of the necessity of maintaining British trade, since tariffs on British goods comprised 70 percent of the federal government's revenue, Washington took advantage of British overtures to dispatch John Jay to London in 1794. Under the treaty Jay negotiated, the United States granted Britain most-favored-nation status in American commerce, promised to prohibit French privateers from operating out of American ports, accepted the British government's broad definition of contraband (war materials, which could not be exported to France), and pledged to pay the pre-Revolutionary debts. In return, the British promised to evacuate the forts in the Ohio valley by 1796 and to pay reparations for American ships seized in 1793-1794.

Republicans were outraged by the Jay Treaty. They called Jay a traitor for cozying up to the recent enemy and predicted that the British would again violate their promise to evacuate the northwestern forts. (They were wrong; this time the British withdrew.) Jay claimed that he could travel across the country at night by the light of his flaming effigies. Washington endorsed the treaty in order to avoid war, and in so doing, brought unprecedented criticism upon himself. The treaty barely secured the two-thirds Senate vote necessary for its ratification, on June 24, 1795.

The Jay Treaty produced strong partisan passions. Jefferson wrote: "Men who have been intimate all their lives cross the street to avoid meeting and turn their heads another way, lest they should be obliged to touch their hats." Foreign policy was intertwined with domestic policy. The "anarchy" of the French radicals represented the Federalists' worst fears of democracy, and they anxiously fingered their own necks when American mobs, supportive of the French radicals, guillotined the effigies of Jay. By contrast, Republicans excused the violence in France as necessary to the overthrow of entrenched monarchy and aristocracy. Jefferson maintained that the tree of liberty must be periodically watered by the blood of tyrants and martyrs. Republicans suspected that the Federalists' pro-British policy represented a love of the same despicable British institutions from which Americans had so recently been freed.

Perhaps the only uncontroversial event of the 1790s was the Pinckney Treaty (also known as the Treaty of San Lorenzo). The treaty was the product of Spain's desire to foster good relations with the United States in order to prevent an attack on Spanish territory by British and American forces. Compelled by French republican victories to abandon their short-lived alliance with Britain, Spanish officials feared that the vengeful British would join with the Americans, with whom they had just reconciled, in an invasion of Spanish Louisiana and Florida. Such fears were exacerbated by American outcries against Spanish restrictions on their "right" to navigate the Mississippi River and by the Treaty of Greenville. In the Treaty of Greenville (August 1795) twelve northwestern Native American tribes had been compelled to cede most of what is now Ohio (as well as enclosures at Detroit, Vincennes, and Chicago) to the United States after being decimated by "Mad Anthony" Wayne and his 2,600 soldiers at Fallen Timbers (August 4, 1794). Fearful of an Anglo-American combination against them, the Spanish adopted a policy of appeasement toward the United States.

In the treaty, negotiated by U.S. Minister to Spain Thomas Pinckney, the Spanish conceded every point. Dropping their claims to land as far north as the Tennessee River, they accepted the Thirty-First Parallel as the northern boundary of Spanish Florida and granted Americans the right to navigate freely the Mississippi River and to deposit goods, free of duty, at New Orleans for three years. The Spanish also promised to pacify the Native Americans within their borders. (Fearful of American expansion, the Spanish had been encouraging Native American attacks on American settlers.) The U.S. Senate ratified the treaty by a large margin.

While both Republicans and Federalists endorsed the territorial expansion wrought by the Pinckney Treaty, they differed dramatically concerning the disposition of western land. In an effort to maintain the United States as a society of small farmers, the Republicans advocated a federal policy of selling western land cheaply and in small parcels. Seeking a more diversified economy, the Federalists advocated the sale of land at high prices and in large lots. The expansion of American industry would require a labor supply that could best be obtained by making western land too expensive for common people to afford. Thus, the Federalists' Land Act of 1796 doubled the price of government land to two dollars per acre, with just one year for complete payment, and stipulated that land be sold only in blocks of eight sections (5,120 acres), so that only a few wealthy speculators could afford it. Before Congress passed this act, three new states, Vermont (1791), Kentucky (1792), and Tennessee (1796), had been added to the Union. But between 1796 and 1800, less than 50,000 acres of federal land was sold. The Republicans' Land Act of 1800 would later reduce the minimum sale to 320 acres and spread payment over four years. Their Land Act of 1804 would go farther, lowering the minimum sale to 160 acres, thenceforth the standard "homestead," and reducing the price to $1.64 per acre.

By siding more with the Federalists during his second term, Washington undermined his popularity among radical Republicans, some of whom accused him of tyranny or senility. Even Washington's old friend Thomas Paine wrote in an open letter (1796): "The world will be puzzled to decide whether you are an apostate or an impostor; whether you have abandoned good principles, or whether you ever had any." Tired of such scurrilous attacks, Washington resigned after two terms, thereby establishing a precedent later formalized by the Twenty-Second Amendment (1951). *The Philadelphia Aurora* declared: "This day ought to be a jubilee in the United States. . . . If ever a nation has been debauched by a man, the American Nation has been debauched by Washington."

Despite Washington's famous warning against political parties in his Farewell Address, his successor John Adams encountered the same factionalism. The unfortunate Adams was immediately beset by conflict with France. Angered by the Jay Treaty, and in desperate need of ships, France had broken off relations with the United States and had seized 300 American vessels by the time of Adams' inauguration in 1797. Adams had tried to smooth relations with France, sending Charles C. Pinckney, John Marshall, and Elbridge Gerry to negotiate. But three agents of French Foreign Minister Charles Maurice de Talleyrand, called "X, Y, and Z" by Adams in his subsequent report to Congress, told the American representatives that they would not negotiate unless the United States loaned France $12 million, gave a $250,000 bribe to the French government's five directors, and apologized for Adams' message to Congress criticizing the French. Bribery was common in the eighteenth century. Even Washington had bribed Creek chieftains and Barbary pirates (the latter for the return of American sailors taken hostage). But Talleyrand's price was exceptionally high, especially for simply agreeing to negotiate.

Americans were outraged. In a famous banquet toast Robert Goodloe Harper summarized popular feeling when he declared: "Millions for defense, but not one cent for tribute." An undeclared naval war between France and the United States erupted (1798) in the Caribbean Sea, in the Mediterranean Sea, and on the Indian Ocean. Congress authorized the seizure of French ships, suspended trade with France, and strengthened American defenses. At Adams' urging Congress also provided for the construction of a fleet of thirty-three warships by 1799. A 10,000-man army was raised and placed under the ostensible control of Washington, though his health was so poor that Alexander Hamilton held effective command. Fearful of French spies, the Federalist Congress even passed the Alien and Sedition Acts (1798), which lengthened immigrants' naturalization period from five to fourteen years, authorized the president to deport aliens he considered dangerous, and imprisoned those who spoke or wrote "false, scandalous, and malicious" words against the government. Rarely enforced, the acts merely created unlikely martyrs among Republican tabloid editors and motivated Madison and Jefferson to draft the Virginia and Kentucky Resolutions (1798), which implied that states could nullify federal laws they considered unconstitutional.

The Election of 1800

In one of the most courageous acts of an exceptionally courageous political career John Adams knowingly sacrificed his re-election for the cause of peace. Adams infuriated Hamilton and his wing of the Federalist Party, whose support he needed for re-election, by negotiating peace with France on October 1, 1800 (in the Convention of Mortefontaine). Adams' negotiations completely undercut Hamiltonian Federalist efforts to create a sizable and permanent military establishment and foiled Hamilton's personal ambition to conquer Spanish territory in Florida, Louisiana, and even South America. (In fairness, Hamilton was partly motivated by the fear that either France or Britain would seize Louisiana from Spain before the

United States could.) Hamilton had long disliked Adams, because Adams had helped persuade Congress to remove Hamilton's father-in-law Philip Schuyler from the patriots' northern command during the Revolutionary War and because Adams had opposed some of Hamilton's fiscal policies. Hamilton had even conspired to deny Adams the presidency in 1796. Angry that Adams had robbed him of his chance to gain military laurels, Hamilton now drafted a pamphlet, intended only for Federalist luminaries, which questioned Adams' leadership ability. The pamphlet fell into the hands of the Republican Aaron Burr, who published it. The Federalist Party was split.

Ironically, the same peace negotiations with France which cost Adams his re-election made it possible for his rival, Thomas Jefferson, to purchase the vast territory of Louisiana from France three years later. Had Adams not made peace with France, the United States would have found itself engaged in an increasingly costly war against a nation now ruled by a military genius. By 1799 the Corsican general Napoleon Bonaparte had become the dictator of France (though he cleverly restricted himself to the republican title of "First Consul"), after deposing the same incompetent and corrupt Directory he had brilliantly defended against both foreign and domestic foes. But the new peace placed the United States and France on friendly terms, thereby allowing Jefferson to reap the glory of the Louisiana Purchase. In 1787 Jefferson had written of Adams: "He is vain, irritable, and a bad calculator of the force and probable effect of the motives that govern men. This is all the ill which can possibly be said of him. He is as disinterested as the Being who made him."

The Republicans nominated Jefferson and Burr. Jefferson drafted the first party platform in American history. The platform emphasized Jefferson's opposition to taxes. Jefferson and Burr defeated Adams 75 to 63 in the Electoral College, with Burr's home state of New York providing the margin of victory. Burr had run a revolutionary campaign in the state.

Unlike most politicians of his aristocratic era, Burr had not been ashamed or afraid to court the common man. He had established ward-by-ward organization, supplied Republican voters with transportation to the polls, and canvassed for funds. He had even attended horse races, cock fights, and "Methodist quarterly meetings."

But something peculiar happened. Under the system established by the Constitution, the electors of the Electoral College were required to write two names on their ballots. Whoever received a majority of the electoral votes became president; whoever received the second most votes became vice-president. The Republicans had intended that Jefferson be president, Burr vice-president. But since they had forgotten to arrange that at least one of the electors withhold a Burr vote, Jefferson and Burr had tied. Since neither had won a majority of the electoral votes, the election then moved to the House of Representatives. Burr shocked Republicans by refusing to concede the election to Jefferson. He believed that he deserved the presidency since he had contributed more than Jefferson to the Republican victory over Adams. Ironically, since Hamilton possessed a great deal of influence in the House, he now played a decisive role in determining which leader of the opposition party would become president. Hamilton disliked Jefferson, but hated and feared Burr, his New York rival. In 1792 Hamilton had written: "In a word, if we have an embryo-Caesar in the United States, 'tis Burr." Against the wishes of some Federalists, who preferred Burr, Hamilton supported Jefferson after the Virginian promised to keep some Federalists in office and to maintain some of Hamilton's fiscal program. After thirty-five ballots, Jefferson won the election. Burr, the second-place finisher, became vice-president. But the new president now regarded his vice-president with understandable suspicion. By separating the presidential and vice-presidential races, the Twelfth Amendment (1804) prevented a recurrence of this fiasco.

The nation held its breath after Jefferson's election. The old Federalist ladies of Boston hid their Bibles, lest this alleged "atheist" send troops into their homes to wrest it from them. Outgoing President John Adams worked feverishly to fill the new judicial positions created by the outgoing Federalist Congress with party members, as a last stronghold against the Virginia "anarchist" who would reduce the nation to chaos. (And Adams and Jefferson had once been close friends!) This was the first transfer of power between political parties in American history. Nowhere else in the world were such transfers accomplished without bloodshed, people noted breathlessly. Would it occur peacefully in the United States?

The Purchase

The first president to be inaugurated in the new federal city of Washington, District of Columbia, Jefferson attempted to calm Federalist fears in his inaugural address. He declared: "We are all Republicans—we are all Federalists. If there be any among us who would wish to dissolve the Union or to change its republican form, let them stand undisturbed as monuments of the safety with which error of opinion may be tolerated where reason is left free to combat it." To the Federalist argument that the federal government lacked the power it needed, Jefferson retorted: "I believe this, on the contrary, the strongest government on earth. I believe it is the only one where every man . . . would meet invasions of the public order as his own personal concern. Sometimes it is said that man cannot be trusted with the government of himself. Can he, then, be trusted with the government of others? Or have we found angels in the form of kings to govern him? Let history answer this question."

But Jefferson soon faced an apparent catastrophe. He learned of the Treaty of San Ildefonso (October 2, 1800), in which Bonaparte had successfully pressured Spanish King Charles IV into retroceding Louisiana to France and

Thomas Jefferson
(Copyrighted by the White House Historical Association.
Photograph by National Geographic Society)

contributing six ships to the French navy. In return Bonaparte had given the Spanish only two face-saving promises: the pledge that the duke of Parma, Charles' son-in-law, would receive Tuscany (in northern Italy) and the promise that Bonaparte would not sell or cede Louisiana to a third party. the First Consul was to violate both pledges. (He placed the duke's son on the Tuscan throne as a figurehead, but retained actual control of the kingdom himself.) In reacquiring Louisiana, Bonaparte was only following the policy pursued by each of the preceding republican governments of France. (The Girondists had instructed Edmond Genet to persuade Americans to help him seize Louisiana by force; the Jacobins and the Directory had negotiated for it. Aware that Spain was losing money on the colony, the Directors had argued that France alone was powerful enough to safeguard Spanish Mexico by ending American expansion: "We alone can trace with [a] strong and respected hand the bounds of the power of the United States and the limits of their territory." But Spain's price had been too high until Bonaparte had issued thinly veiled threats of another French invasion of Spain.)

Most Americans were alarmed by the news that neighboring Louisiana would pass from weak Spain to powerful France. As Jefferson had put it, in 1786: "Our confederacy must be viewed as the nest from which all America, North and South, is to be peopled. We should take care not to think it for the interest of that great continent to press too soon on the Spaniards. Those countries cannot be in better hands." He had feared only that Spain might be "too feeble" to hold Louisiana until the population of the United States became "sufficiently advanced to gain it from them piece by piece." In the 1790s, while secretary of state, Jefferson had encouraged Americans to accept Spanish offers to settle in Louisiana in exchange for an oath of allegiance to Spain, saying: "It will be the means of delivering to us peaceably what may otherwise cost us a war." (The Spanish were pursuing the same foolish policy as the late Roman emperors, who had allowed Germanic tribes of dubious loyalty to settle in the empire as a barrier against other Germanic tribes. The wily Jefferson had even suggested to President Washington: "In the meantime we may complain of this seduction of our inhabitants just enough to make them [the Spanish] believe we think it a very wise policy for them and confirm them in it.") But such hopes of having the Louisiana apple fall ripe from the Spanish tree into the American lap were foiled by Spain's retrocession of the colony to France. Even Jefferson, who despised Great Britain, had declared only a few years earlier: "The day that France takes possession of New Orleans . . . we must marry ourselves to the British fleet and nation." A shotgun wedding, to be sure.

Jefferson immediately appointed Robert Livingston U.S. Minister to France and dispatched him to Paris with a set of instructions. If the rumored retrocession had not yet occurred, Livingston was to threaten an alliance with Great Britain if France went ahead with it. If the retrocession had occurred, Livingston was to insist on purchasing New Orleans and Florida, which Jefferson mistakenly believed had been included in the retrocession, for $2 million.

The situation became even more critical for the United States while Livingston negotiated. In October of 1802, Juan Ventura Morales, the acting intendant of Spanish Louisiana (the Spanish had delayed the colony's retrocession to the French), received instructions from Charles IV, who was alarmed by American economic penetration of Louisiana. Acting on these secret orders, Morales suspended Americans' right of deposit at New Orleans. The economies of the western states were desperately dependent on access to New Orleans as a place of deposit. Before western grain could be shipped to the Atlantic coast, the West Indies, and western Europe, it must be unloaded from riverboats into warehouses on the lower Mississippi River, to await the arrival of ocean-going vessels. Although the Spanish did not restrict American navigation of the lower Mississippi, so that American ships could still unload

James Monroe

Painting attributed to James Herring
(Courtesy National Portrait Gallery, Smithsonian Institution)

Robert R. Livingston
(Courtesy Collection of The New-York Historical Society)

directly onto ocean-going ships in New Orleans, and American merchants could even get around the deposit restrictions by operating through Spanish nationals in the city, westerners were frantic with the fear that Bonaparte was working through the Spanish to destroy their vibrant economy. Some westerners spoke of invading Louisiana. Others, furious at the eastern elite which dominated the federal government for allegedly ignoring their concerns, seriously considered secession from the United States and a pact with Spain if the federal government could not secure them a place of deposit on the lower Mississippi. (Ironically, the South was the last section of the Union to consider secession. Federalist New England considered secession just a few years after the West, while bitterly opposed to the War of 1812. Ironically, John C. Calhoun, the leading state rights advocate of the antebellum South, learned state rights theory while studying at Yale just before that war.)

Alarmed by talk of western secession, Jefferson lost no opportunity to reiterate to France, both directly and through Secretary of State James Madison, the threat of an Anglo-American alliance if the French took possession of New Orleans. This was no bluff. Jefferson considered Louisiana so vital to the survival of the Union that he was prepared to form a military alliance with the hated British to secure it. Jefferson wrote: "There is on the globe one single spot the possessor of which is our natural and habitual enemy. It is New Orleans, through which the produce of three eighths of our territory must pass to market." He noted: "Every eye in the U.S. is now fixed on this affair of Louisiana. Perhaps nothing since the revolutionary war has produced more uneasy sensations through the body of the nation." Jefferson concentrated militia at Fort Adams, thirty-eight miles south of Natchez, in the event that an attack on New Orleans should become necessary. He also purchased land along the Mississippi from Native American tribes in order to increase the number of American settlers on the frontier.

In January of 1803 Jefferson dispatched James Monroe as a special emissary to France in order to placate westerners and to impress Bonaparte with the seriousness of the crisis. Jefferson authorized Monroe to raise the American offer for New Orleans and Florida to $9,375,000. If the French refused to sell, Monroe must at least demand deposit rights. If the French refused deposit rights, Monroe was to proceed to London and discuss a possible alliance with Great Britain. In the event of war with France Jefferson considered a British alliance necessary. The United States might be able to seize New Orleans unassisted, but it could not thwart a French blockade alone.

Livingston resented Monroe's commission, considering it a manifestation of Jefferson's lack of confidence in him. By the time Monroe arrived in Paris (April 12) Livingston was already deeply involved in negotiations with French Foreign Minister Talleyrand, one of the most intriguing men (no pun intended) of the eighteenth and nineteenth centuries. Talleyrand was a master conniver whose political cunning enabled him to survive the bloodiest and most chaotic period in French history. By shifting with the political winds, Talleyrand had survived the turmoil and executions of revolutionary France. Like a cat, Talleyrand always landed on his feet (even as a child, when his nurse dropped him). Because his deformed foot had precluded a military career, his parents had sent him to a seminary. Although Talleyrand had been ordained a Roman Catholic bishop, his taste for women and intrigue had naturally led him into diplomacy, where he had made himself indispensable to successive governments. For two years during the Reign of Terror he had lived as an exile in the United States and had become a friend of Alexander Hamilton. Talleyrand had been miserable in a relatively quiet, frugal, republican country like the United States and had missed the intrigues of French politics. He complained: "In America I found thirty-one religions and only one dish." (By contrast, a truly civilized country like France possessed only one religion and at least

Charles-Maurice de Talleyrand

(Courtesy Portrait File, Miriam and Ira D. Wallach Division of Art, Prints, and Photographs
The New York Public Library
Astor, Lenox and Tilden Foundations)

Napoleon Bonaparte
(Courtesy The Historic New Orleans Collections, Museum/Research Center, Acc. No. 199.34.19)

thirty-one dishes.) Fortunately for Talleyrand, both the Directory and Bonaparte had use for him in France (partly because they liked his idea of reviving France's New World Empire). As we have seen, in 1798 Talleyrand had helped start an undeclared war with the United States by demanding bribes for himself and the Directors, a rare miscalculation on the foreign minister's part. In assuming that the American commissioners would consider the bribes a mere business expense, he had failed to take American moralism into account. Worse yet, in charging unreasonable prices, he had failed to take American frugality into account.

Fortunately, the United States' secession crisis abated. On March 1, Charles IV ordered Morales to restore the American right to deposit at New Orleans. With the war in Europe about to resume, Spain did not want to wage a second war against the United States on behalf of a colony it would soon be forced to relinquish. Although Spain's capable administration of Louisiana and recruitment of new settlers, such as the Acadians, had reduced the colony's annual cost from $1,500,000 to $500,000 and had raised the colony's population from 8,000 to 50,000, Louisiana was still far too weak to fulfill its historic purpose of checking American expansion.

Better yet for the United States, in April Bonaparte surprised Livingston by acceding to the American diplomat's unauthorized proposal that France sell all of Louisiana to the United States. Bonaparte had reached the decision to sell the vast colony the previous month as the result of a slave rebellion in French St. Domingue (Haiti) which had already lasted a decade. Led by the brilliant Toussaint L'Ouverture (who, ironically, liked being called the "Bonaparte of the Antilles"), the slaves, aided by an epidemic of yellow fever, had successfully waged a guerilla campaign against French troops. In 1802 they had decimated an expeditionary force led by Bonaparte's brother-in-law Charles Leclerc. Leclerc himself had succumbed to the fever. After surveying the situation, his replacement, General Donatien de Rochambeau, had called for

35,000 more troops. By mid-March, when Bonaparte had reached his decision, 50,000 French soldiers had died in St. Domingue.

In his decision to sell all of Louisiana Bonaparte had taken three factors into account: that he could not afford to lose the lucrative sugar colony of St. Domingue, "the jewel of France's colonies"; that since Louisiana was practically worthless without New Orleans, the two should not be separated in any deal; and that he was about to renew the war against Great Britain which had been suspended by the Treaty of Amiens the previous year. His recent losses in Haiti meant that he could no longer hope to defend both Haiti and Louisiana against the British while at the same time reviving his quest for territory in the Mediterranean basin (Malta and Egypt). Under these circumstances, did it not make sense to sell Louisiana to the anti-British Jefferson administration? Bonaparte had been influenced in this matter by the Haitian planters in his entourage and by his wife, Josephine, a lady of Martinique lineage who owned a plantation in St. Domingue. But his reasoning was quite logical. As he put it: "They only ask of me one town in Louisiana, but I already consider the colony as entirely lost, and it appears to me that in the hands of this growing power, it will be more useful to the policy and even to the commerce of France, than if I should attempt to keep it. . . . This accession of territory strengthens forever the power of the United States; and I have just given England a maritime rival that will sooner or later humble her pride." Bonaparte told Talleyrand: "I will not keep a possession which will not be safe in our hands, that may perhaps embroil me with the Americans, or may place me in a state of coolness with them. I shall make it serve me, on the contrary, to attach them to me, to get them into differences with the English, and I shall create for them [the English] enemies who will one day avenge us, if we do not succeed in avenging ourselves. My resolution is fixed; I will give Louisiana to the United States. But as they have no territory to cede to me in exchange, I shall demand of them a sum of money to pay the expenses of the extraordinary armament I am projecting against Great Britain." To return Louisiana to Spain, whose deliberate delay tactics had already angered Bonaparte, would be to give it to the United States, anyway, since Spain was too weak to hold it. It was better to have American friendship and compensation than to lose the colony to the United States or Great Britain in an expensive war.

The Haitian rebellion's crucial role in the Louisiana Purchase is filled with irony. The same rebellion which led to Louisiana's incorporation into the United States also contributed greatly to the distinctiveness of the state's culture. White refugees and black slaves from Haiti contributed most of the state's distinctive food and much of its present culture. Furthermore, it is ironic that the same slave rebellion Jefferson regarded with fear and loathing secured for him his greatest personal dream and his greatest presidential achievement. The story ends less fortunately for Toussaint, however. Fooled by an agreement which offered the slaves their freedom under French rule and Toussaint a general's commission in the French army, Toussaint surrendered himself. He was deported to a French prison, where he died of pneumonia and maltreatment.

But Toussaint's rebellion only forced upon Bonaparte a larger realization long shared by American leaders and more recently forced upon the Spanish. Although four powers contended for Louisiana—Great Britain, France, Spain, and the United States—only the United States was free of European concerns; only the United States could devote its whole, rapidly growing power and energy to North American expansion. Hence, no European colony was ultimately safe from the United States. The United States was destined, by the realities of power if not by God, to rule the continent.

Bonaparte's decision was unpopular in France. The British had bribed his two brothers Joseph and Lucien to oppose the sale in order to keep Napoleon's attention focused on the New World and away from Europe (particularly Malta, which the

British had agreed to cede to France under the Treaty of Amiens, but from which they now refused to withdraw). The brothers engaged Napoleon in a heated discussion while he was bathing. When Joseph threatened to lead the legislative opposition to the sale, an enraged Napoleon laughed derisively and fell back in the tub, drenching Joseph. Since Talleyrand had also been bribed to oppose the sale, Napoleon placed the negotiations in the hands of François Barbé-Marbois, who had a reputation for honesty (unlike Talleyrand) and who had married an American woman.

On April 30, 1803, American and French delegates initialed the treaty. The United States agreed to purchase Louisiana for $11.25 million and $3.75 million in American claims against the French government. For twelve years French and Spanish ships would pay no higher duty in Louisiana ports than American vessels. The inhabitants of Louisiana would be given full citizenship under the U.S. Constitution as soon as possible.

Few could deny that Livingston and Monroe had negotiated a good bargain. Under the treaty the United States would purchase the whole western Mississippi River valley, 828,000 square miles, for about three cents per acre. (Only Texans consider it a bad deal.) Livingston remarked: "We have lived long, but this is the noblest work of our whole lives. . . . From this day the United States take their place among the powers of the first rank. . . . The instruments which we have just signed will cause no tears to be shed: they prepare ages of happiness for innumerable generations of human creatures." Livingston had good reason to be proud. He had overcome his deafness, his inability to speak French, and his resentment of Monroe to negotiate the most important treaty in American history. On May 18, less than three weeks after the treaty was initialed, Great Britain declared war against France when Bonaparte refused to withdraw from the Netherlands.

The treaty was vague in defining Louisiana's northern boundary with British Canada, its southeastern border with

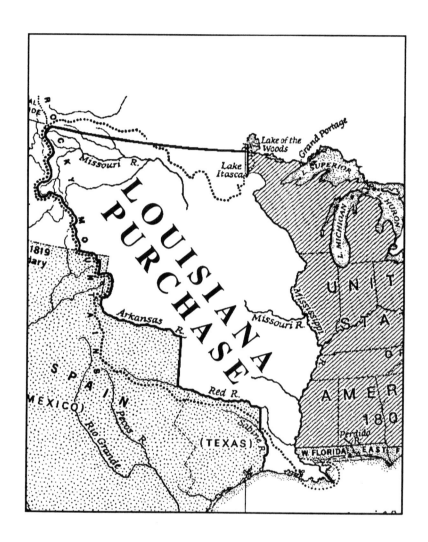

Spanish Florida, and its southwestern boundary with Spanish Texas. When Livingston asked about the borders, Talleyrand's response was typically, but prophetically, cynical: "I can give you no direction. You have made a noble bargain for yourselves, and I suppose you will make the most of it." In case Talleyrand's statement was too subtle for slow-witted Americans Bonaparte added: "If an obscurity did not exist, perhaps it would be good policy to put it there."

Jefferson was in agony and ecstasy. He was in ecstasy because he believed that the vast and fertile soil of Louisiana would ensure that the United States would continue to pursue his vision of a society of small farmers for centuries. Since the 1780s Jefferson's interest in Louisiana had led him to support its exploration. In fact, immediately after his inauguration in 1801, Jefferson had dispatched his twenty-nine-year-old secretary, Meriwether Lewis, to explore the West to the Pacific Ocean—despite the fact that France and Spain denied the president permission to send explorers through their territory. Lewis had then chosen William Clark to assist him. In addition to their other research duties Jefferson instructed the explorers to engage in military reconnaissance, in case an invasion of Louisiana should become necessary. (Fortunately for the explorers, the Louisiana Purchase was concluded just before they departed.) Jefferson even envisioned American ports on the Pacific Ocean which would permit a lucrative trade with Asia, a dream which had not died since the day Christopher Columbus had set sail for that continent. Furthermore, Jefferson was relieved that Louisiana could be acquired without war, though he considered the stakes high enough to warrant the use of force if necessary. Expansion, even by war, was proper if the inhabitants of the new territories eventually received equal representation. This principle, which distinguished American expansion from European colonialism, had been enshrined in Jefferson's Northwest Ordinance of 1787. In addition, the wild celebrations which accompanied news of the treaty testified to its popularity and, hence, to its potential benefit to the Republican Party.

But Jefferson was simultaneously in agony because he understood that the treaty contradicted the strict constructionism he championed. In fact, Jefferson's first thought was to call for a constitutional amendment to allow the purchase, but his advisors wisely warned that by the time such an amendment was ratified by three-quarters of the states the restless Bonaparte might change his mind about the sale. Furthermore, the power to purchase territory, they argued in Federalist fashion, was implied in the power of the executive to negotiate treaties. Secretary of the Treasury Albert Gallatin wrote: "The existence of the United States as a nation presupposes the power enjoyed by every nation of extending their territory by treaties and the general power given to the President and Senate of making treaties designates the organs through which the acquisition may be made." But Jefferson disagreed: "The general government has no powers but such as the constitution has given it; and it has not given it a power of holding foreign territory and still less of incorporating it into the Union." But, alarmed by news of Bonaparte's impatience, Jefferson reluctantly decided to abandon one of the most sacred principles of the Republican Party, strict construction of the Constitution, and to support the treaty. In a remarkable statement of surrender Jefferson was reduced to the hope "that the good sense of our country will correct the evil of loose construction when it shall produce ill effects." He justified the decision by its positive benefits: "The world will here see such an extent of country under a free and moderate government as it has never yet seen."

Pastoralism: The Genealogy of an Idea

Anyone who would understand how Jefferson could have surrendered so crucial a principle as the strict interpretation of the Constitution must understand his even greater emotional attachment to the classical tradition of pastoralism. No theme was more ubiquitous in Greco-Roman literature than that of the superiority of the rural, agricultural existence, a lifestyle wedged comfortably between the extremes of "savage" and "sophisticated." A motif of some Greek poets, like Hesiod and Theocritus, pastoralism became the central theme of Virgil, Horace, and Ovid, the leading poets of Rome's Augustan Age. Convinced that farmers were the backbone of Rome, Virgil's *Georgics* (2.458-474) exhorted his fellow Romans to regenerate the community after a century of civil war by returning to the plow:

> How lucky the farmers are—I wish they knew!
> The Earth herself, most just, pours forth for them
> An easy living from the soil, far off
> From clashing weapons, though the farmer has
> No mansion with proud portals which spits out
> A monster wave of morning visitors
> From every room, nor do his callers gasp
> At inlaid columns, bright with tortoiseshell,
> Or gold-embroidered clothes or bronzes from
> Ephyre, nor in his house is plain white wool
> Dyed with Assyrian poison, nor does he
> Corrupt his olive oil with foreign spice,
> He has untroubled sleep and honest life.
> Rich in all sorts of riches, with a vast
> Estate, he has all the leisure to enjoy
> A cave, a natural pond, a valley where
> The air is cool—the mooing of the cows
> Is ever present, and to sleep beneath
> A tree is sweet. Wild animals abound
> For hunting, and young people grow up strong,
> Hardworking, satisfied with poverty:
> Their gods are holy; parents are revered.
> Surely, when Justice left the earth she stayed
> Last with these folk, and left some tokens here.
> The farmer's lifestyle was the source of republican virtue.

The pastoral theme was as much as a staple of classical political theory and history as of Greco-Roman poetry. Aristotle argued that the best republics were predominantly agricultural. The classical historians Polybius, Plutarch, Livy,

Tacitus, and Sallust considered Sparta and republican Rome models not merely because they had possessed mixed governments, but also because they had been agricultural societies. These historians credited the triumph of Sparta and Rome over their vice-ridden, commercial adversaries, Athens and Carthage, as much to their pastoral virtues as to their government forms. Both produced virtue, the agricultural life by fostering frugality, temperance, and independence, the balanced constitution by encouraging moderation, cooperation, and compromise. The plow was both the symbol and the cause of Cincinnatus' "Roman virtue." Furthermore, classical historians attributed the downfall of the Roman republic to "the Punic Curse," the commercialization of Rome which had resulted from the republic's conquest of the Carthaginian empire. The curse of commercial wealth had transformed Rome from a modest village into an imperial city. Whether by choice or necessity, farmers had abandoned the soil for the iniquitous life of the city. Deprived of that dignity which an independent means of sustenance affords the farmer, these former bastions of republicanism had become the clients of dictators, prepared to sell the once-glorious republic for the paltry price of bread and circuses. Disgruntled by their forced subservience to the emperors, the aristocratic poets and historians who painted this compelling portrait idealized an epoch which their class had dominated, though their own luxurious lifestyles would hardly have suited them to the rustic existence their works immortalized. Like most worshipers of agriculture who succeeded them, the Roman pastoralists lived a life distant from the manual labor they extolled. Far less romantic about their lot, many of the farmers the pastoralists glorified preferred the freedom from "noble toil" which life in the city afforded—hence Virgil's need to tell the farmers how lucky they were. As in the case of mixed government, these Roman aristocrats offered an ideal whose simple beauty remains powerful, however unreflective of reality and however self-interested in origin.

The founders derived the pastoral tradition both directly from the ancients, who formed the core of their grammar school and college curricula, and through the medium of modern authors. Having spread throughout the Middle Ages and the Renaissance, pastoralism achieved a virtual cult status in seventeenth- and eighteenth-century England and France. The political philosopher James Harrington praised farmers for their love of liberty, moderated by a stability which he found lacking in the city-dwellers of Athens. An enthusiastic supporter of agriculture, King George III was fond of the nickname "Farmer George." Both Farmer Georges, the king and the rebel Washington, corresponded with Arthur Young, one of the high priests of the eighteenth-century pastoral movement. Young declared: "Perhaps we might, without any great impropriety, call farming the reigning taste of the present times."

Thomas Jefferson cherished the pastoral tradition even more than most of his contemporaries. His favorite books on agriculture were Columella's *De re rustica* and Adam Dickson's *Husbandry of the Ancients.* Like other Virginia aristocrats, Jefferson designed his estate, Monticello, to resemble the Roman villas Pliny the Younger and Varro had described. He also planned the inscription of a Latin passage from Horace (*Epodes*, 2.1-4, 7-8, 23-34, 39-40, 43-48, 61-66) near a small temple which he hoped to build on his burial ground. The excerpt, which he had copied into his notebook as a young man, exulted:

> Happy the man who, free from business worries, like the men of the old days, tills with his oxen his ancestral fields without being harassed by mortgages. . . . He keeps away from the Forum and the proud threshold of the powers that be. . . . He likes to recline now under an ancient oak, now on the thick grass. Meanwhile the brooks flow between the high banks, birds warble in the woods, and springs bubble with running water, a sweet invitation to repose. But when the wintry season of thundering Jove brings back rains and snows, either with his pack of hounds he drives the fierce boars into the traps, or arranges large meshed nets on polished sticks to snare the greedy thrushes; . . . If a

modest wife, who does her part in tending the house and her dear
children piles high the sacred hearth with dry firewood waiting for
the return of her tired husband, gathers in a pen made of wattles
the fat ewes in order to milk their distended udders, and drawing
from the keg new sweet wine, prepares a meal which she had not
to pay for . . . amid such feasts what joy to see the tired oxen
dragging along the upturned ploughshare and the young slaves,
industrious swarm of an opulent house, seated around the
resplendent Lares.

As Gilbert Chinard noted, Jefferson removed from the text
of Horace's epode those parts which described elements absent
from eighteenth-century Virginia life (shrill war clarions and
vineyards, for instance). By condensing a poem of seventy-two
lines into thirty-two, he presented a picture, however idealized,
of his own time and place. By 1819 Jefferson was inclined to
write in Latin of "the bond of the sweet natal soil."

Though certainly aware of economic arguments for the
greater productivity of agriculture, Jefferson generally
emphasized its moral and political benefits. Jefferson knew
that the French Physiocrats had demonstrated the superior
efficiency of large plantations, but he continued to champion
the small farm. In a famous passage in the *Notes on the State
of Virginia* Jefferson glorified agriculture in a manner
reminiscent of the *Georgics*:

> Those who labor in the earth are the chosen people of God, if
> ever He had a chosen people, whose breasts He has made His
> peculiar deposit for genuine and substantial virtue. He keeps alive
> that sacred fire, which otherwise might escape from the face of the
> earth. Corruption of morals in the mass of cultivators is a
> phenomenon of which no age nor nation has furnished an example.
> It is the mark set on those, who, not looking up to heaven and to
> their own soil and industry as does the husbandman, for their
> subsistence, depend for it on casualties and caprices of customers.
> Dependence begets subservience and venality suffocates the germ
> of virtue and prepares fit tools for the designs of ambition. . . . The
> mobs of great cities add just so much to the support of pure
> government as sores do to the strength of the human body. It is the
> manners and spirit of a people which preserves a republic in vigor.
> A degeneracy in these is a canker which soon eats to the heart of
> its laws and constitution.

The secret of the ancient republics' success was their pastoral societies. Jefferson later wrote: "Cultivators of the earth are the most valuable citizens. They are the most vigorous, the most independent, the most virtuous, and they are tied to their country, and wedded to its liberty and interests by the most lasting bonds. . . . I consider the class of artificers as the panders of vice, and the instruments by which the liberties of a country are overturned."

Jefferson's passionate attachment to the pastoral tradition colored his perceptions of the world. The Virginian frequently compared the British commercialism he detested with that of the Carthaginians, implying an analogy between the United States and the frugal Roman republic. In 1810 he scoffed at the suggestion of an alliance with Great Britain: "The faith of a nation of merchants! The *Punica fides* of modern Carthage." Later that year, after predicting a mutiny in the British navy, Jefferson further claimed that if the mutineers could not establish a military dictatorship, they would become individual pirates, and "the modern Carthage will end as the old one has done"—a reference to the Barbary pirates of North Africa. In 1815, a few months after the end of the War of 1812, Jefferson turned from predictions of doom to threats of violence. If the modern Carthage, Great Britain, did not stop injuring the United States, she would force Americans to adopt the famous motto of Cato the Elder, who had ended all his speeches in the Roman senate with: "Carthago delenda est!"—"Carthage must be destroyed!" Jefferson added a dark reference to the brilliant Roman general Scipio Africanus, who had issued a lethal blow to Carthage at Zama in 202 B.C.: "And some Scipio Americanus will leave to posterity the problem of conjecturing where stood once the ancient and splendid city of London." In 1813 and 1815 Jefferson used Cato's motto against the Federalist financial interests that profited from the national debt. He was determined to prevent his Federalist adversaries from transforming the frugal Rome of the United States into another modern Carthage like Britain. Ironically, his very hatred of the modern Carthage forced him, however reluctantly, to adopt some of her policies. After the War of 1812 Jefferson reluctantly recognized that the United States would have to possess some industry in order to maintain its independence from British manufacturers. But Jefferson remained optimistic as long as agriculture held the predominant position in his nation's economy and social life.

In 1803 Jefferson's pastoralism manifested itself in his determination to purchase Louisiana, whatever the constitutional consequences. His desire to recreate the virtuous Roman republic overrode his fear that the federal government might be dangerously empowered by so prominent a violation of strict construction. Jefferson was so determined to perpetuate the agricultural character of the United States that he was willing to violate one of the core principles of the Republican Party in order to purchase Louisiana. When the absence of a constitutional provision allowing Jefferson to buy foreign territory threatened the future of the republic's agricultural base, and hence its virtue and longevity, Jefferson reluctantly sacrificed constitutional scruples in order to extend the life of the republic. Jefferson predicted: "I think our governments will remain virtuous for many centuries; as long as they are chicfly agricultural; and this will be as long as there shall be vacant lands in any part of America."

Ironically, the same pastoralism that excited dread and sorrow in Jefferson's favorite classical poets and historians inspired hope and confidence in the Virginian. Jefferson estimated that 350 years must pass before the vast lands of the West were fully settled. (He could not imagine the revolution in transportation technology and the massive European immigration to the United States which would combine to settle the continent in less than a century.) Hence the same ideology which evoked nostalgia from the imperial literati of Rome could be a source of encouragement to an American sitting on the edge of a fertile and sparsely settled continent.

Ratification

The Louisiana Purchase presented the Federalist Party with
a grave political crisis. As ardent in their desire for territorial
expansion as their Republican opponents, most Federalists
could not have brought themselves to oppose the purchase even
if it had not been wildly popular. They too belonged to a
centuries-old tradition of expansionism. Upon hearing rumors
of a British attempt to seize Louisiana in 1789, Hamilton had
written: "[When] we are able to make good our pretensions,
we ought not to leave in the possession of any foreign power
the territories at the mouth of the Mississippi, which are to be
regarded as the key to it." Nearly a decade later he had
reiterated regarding Louisiana and Florida: "I have been long
in the habit of considering the acquisition of those countries as
essential to the permanency of the Union, which I consider
very important to the welfare of the whole." On the issue of
keeping control of the Mississippi out of the hands of both
Britain and France, and even on the broader issue of territorial
expansion itself, Hamilton stood with his nemesis, Jefferson.
Both also agreed that western secessionism posed a dire threat
to the Union, a threat which could be eliminated only by the
nation's acquisition of the land along the lower Mississippi
River.

As heirs to the expansionist tradition, most Federalists
supported the treaty, but attempted to deny Jefferson any credit
for it. Hamilton recognized that while territorial expansion
might lead to labor shortages in his beloved factories in the
short-term, as potential laborers sought to settle the new
western lands, over time such territorial gains would provide
the resources necessary to make the United States a great
industrial power. Nevertheless, he attributed the purchase to
good fortune "and not to any wise or vigorous measures on the
part of the American government."

Some Federalists even criticized the president for
purchasing Louisiana rather than seizing it. Although

Louisiana was a good bargain, $15 million (counting claims) was a tremendous expenditure for a nation whose Gross Domestic Product was only $10 million. Federalists noted that fifteen million silver dollars piled in a column would extend three miles into the air.

Only a few, anti-expansionist Federalists (mostly from New England) opposed the acquisition of Louisiana. They often used Montesquieu's old argument that a republic must remain small if it wished to remain a republic. This was a peculiar argument coming from the same Federalists who had supported the Constitution on the grounds that Montesquieu was incorrect. Federalist use of Montesquieu's argument was made all the more peculiar by the vast extent of the United States even without Louisiana. Indeed, Jefferson borrowed a theory from his old friend Madison to refute Montesquieu's contention. Jefferson wrote: "I know that the acquisition of Louisiana has been disapproved by some from a candid apprehension that the enlargement of our territory would endanger its union. But who can limit the extent to which the federative principle may operate effectively? The larger our association the less will it be shaken by local passions."

On October 20, 1803, only ten days before the deadline for ratification stipulated in the treaty itself, the U.S. Senate ratified the treaty, 24-7. Bonaparte, meanwhile, had wasted no time approving his own treaty. (He did not trust the French legislature to ratify it.) On November 30 Spain finally transferred Louisiana to France in a ceremony at the Place d'Armes, a public square in New Orleans. On December 20, the French agent Pierre Clément de Laussat formally transferred the colony to the American representatives William C. C. Claiborne and General James Wilkinson in a second ceremony at the same site. Most Creole observers remained silent; a few sobbed. Laussat himself wept, though he quickly recovered and hosted a party for the Americans. On March 10, 1804, Amos Stoddard, a U.S. Army officer, took possession of Upper Louisiana for the United States.

Pierre Clément de Laussat
(Courtesy Collection of the Louisiana State Museum)

William C. C. Claiborne
(Courtesy Collection of the Louisiana State Museum)

45

Artist's Conception of the Ceremony of Transfer
New Orleans, December 20, 1803
*(Courtesy the Louisiana Historical Society
from the Collection of the Louisiana State Museum)*

The Reaction in Louisiana

The small number of Anglo-Americans in New Orleans were jubilant. Most of the 25,000 African-Americans (mostly slaves) regarded the transfer with indifference, as did thousands of Native Americans. But Spanish officials in Louisiana were shocked by France's treachery in violating the Treaty of San Ildefonso by selling Louisiana to a nation which was likely to threaten Spanish Florida and Mexico in the future. These officials were dissuaded from blocking the cession only by American threats to retaliate by attacking both Louisiana and Florida. Finally, most of Louisiana's 25,000 white colonists were shocked and horrified by the Louisiana Purchase. Though long engaged in a burgeoning, illicit trade with the United States, these Louisianians feared that the virulently anti-Catholic Americans would assault their religion and culture. Many Louisianians claimed they would prefer a return to Spanish rule to citizenship in the American republic. Some spoke of flight. The United States government was so concerned about a possible rebellion it issued an "Address to the People of New Orleans" warning them not to join the Spanish officials in the rumored resistance to "our dominion or opposition to its course." The proclamation claimed, "It is your peculiar happiness . . . [to come under the rule] of a philosopher who prefers justice to conquest," but who would not allow any injury to American rights. The address concluded: "Your alternative is clear, for it consists only in making your small district either a field of war or a garden of peace."

Although white Louisianians did not resist the transfer, they soon became distressed by Jefferson's unwillingness to grant them the speedy self-government he had promised in the purchase treaty. While Jefferson would not go as far as some Federalist extremists, who wanted Louisiana reduced to the status of a perpetual colony, the president shared their doubts concerning native Louisianians' capacity for self-government, noting that the latter were accustomed to the rule of dictatorial French and Spanish governors. Jefferson's cautious policy was also motivated by a fear of rebellion (perhaps recalling the Rebellion of 1768, in which some of Louisiana's French settlers had rebelled against the new Spanish regime). Hence, when Congress divided Louisiana into the Territory of Orleans (what is now the state of Louisiana) and the District of Louisiana (the rest of the Louisiana Purchase territory), it gave the president's appointees complete power over both. When Creoles sought statehood for the Territory of Orleans in 1804, noting that the territory possessed the requisite population, Jefferson persuaded Congress to deny their request, writing: "The principles of a popular Government are utterly beyond their comprehension." He added that native Louisianians were "as yet as incapable of self-government as children" and that not one in fifty could "understand the English language." The Territory of Orleans continued under the dictatorial rule of Jefferson's appointees, while critics inveighed against this dangerous departure from republican practice. One Federalist noted, with bitter irony: "After complaining of the excessive power of poor old Adams, they made the modest Jefferson despot of Louisiana."

But, once assured of the stability of American rule in Louisiana, Jefferson moved to placate white Louisianians through a large degree of local self-government and religious toleration. His effort succeeded. In 1806 Louisianians made no move to join Aaron Burr's conspiracy to detach the West from the United States. In 1815, bolstered by Louisiana's new statehood (approved by Congress in 1812), the Creoles proved instrumental to Andrew Jackson's defense of New Orleans against a large British invasion force. Indeed, contrary to popular myth, it was largely the Creole artillerymen, not the Tennessee and Kentucky riflemen, who decimated Edwin Pakenham's veteran soldiers at New Orleans. (2,000 British soldiers were slaughtered, including Pakenham himself, whose body, pickled in a barrel of rum, was returned to his wife aboard ship in the Gulf of Mexico.) By 1815 white Louisianians no longer considered themselves a conquered people. They now considered themselves citizens of a young, but rapidly growing, republic. Though they still clung to their unique culture, they began to see themselves as Americans as well.

The Effects of the Louisiana Purchase

The Louisiana Purchase was among the most significant events in American history. First, it laid the foundations for the United States' world power in the twentieth century by more than doubling the nation's size. Larger than all the western European nations combined, Louisiana provided what became the most productive farmland in the world. It also increased American power by encouraging the leaders of the United States to pursue more vigorously the dream of a nation spanning from ocean to ocean. In 1819 the United States intimidated Spain, then wracked by colonial rebellions throughout Central and South America, into ceding what remained of Florida. (The United States had already annexed West Florida from the Mississippi to the Pearl River in 1810 and from the Pearl to the Perdido in 1813.) In 1845 the United States annexed Texas, a province of Mexico, populated mostly by Anglo-Americans, which had rebelled and formed itself into an independent republic. In 1846 the United States agreed with Great Britain to divide the huge Oregon Country at the Forty-Ninth Parallel, retaining what are now Washington, Oregon, and Idaho. In 1848, having won the Mexican War, the United States forced Mexico to cede California and the rest of what is now the southwestern United States (40 percent of Mexican territory). At the end of the century the United States purchased Alaska from Russia (1867), seized Hawaii from its natives (1898), and captured Puerto Rico, Guam, and the Philippines in the Spanish-American War (1898). In short, the Louisiana Purchase, so important in itself, reinforced the

American belief in the United States' mission to expand in order to spread the blessings of republicanism throughout the continent. By 1900, after the Industrial Revolution had granted Americans the technological means to harvest the nation's vast resources, the United States had become the greatest economic power in the world. By contrast, if the Louisiana Purchase Treaty had not been negotiated and ratified, the western states, so desperately dependent on the Mississippi River, might have seceded, in which case the United States might now consist of only the land east of the Appalachian Mountains.

Second, the Louisiana Purchase helped destroy the doctrine of strict construction of the Constitution, eventually allowing an enormous expansion of federal power. Although the ratification of the Louisiana Purchase Treaty did not completely end strict construction, its supporters were sorely demoralized by the abdication of Jefferson, its most fervent and most renowned advocate. Furthermore, the very popularity and benign effects of the purchase tended to encourage even conservative politicians to put aside constitutional scruples in other, less justifiable, instances. Of course, the power of the federal government was heightened by the rise of Big Business, the Great Depression, the world wars, and the Cold War. Each of these developments presented problems for an enlarged and empowered federal government to solve. But it was the triumph of loose construction which made possible the idea of a federal solution to these problems. The immense federal power of the twentieth century would not have been possible under strict construction, since many of the federal government's modern powers, though now considered routine functions, are not specifically granted by the Constitution.

Third, the Louisiana Purchase helped keep the United States an agricultural nation. Although the North American continent was settled far faster than Jefferson could imagine, and the United States did gradually transform itself into the kind of urban, European-style, industrialized society Jefferson so feared, the nation's formative years would be spent on the farm. Hence, even after the onset of industrialization and urbanization American values remained largely rural and conservative. Most Americans have remained more suspicious of government, more moralistic, and more religious than their European counterparts, though some social critics fear that these values have eroded in the last thirty years.

Fourth, the Louisiana Purchase helped destroy the Federalist Party. The immense popularity of the treaty, combined with its enormous influence in maintaining the agricultural nature of the United States, proved a bonanza for the Republican Party and a blight upon the Federalist Party. The year after the treaty was ratified Jefferson defeated the Federalist Charles C. Pinckney in a landslide, 162 to 14 electoral votes. Pinckney won only Connecticut and Delaware. The farmers who settled the West supported the Republican Party. The resultant labor shortage in northeastern factories not only delayed the Federalist dream of an industrial United States, but deprived the party of essential support. The Federalist Party was further weakened by the loss of leadership which occurred when Washington died (1799), Adams retired (1801), and Burr killed Hamilton in a duel (1804) and by the Republicans' outright theft of parts of the Federalist program. The final blow to the party was the Hartford Convention (1814), at which radical Federalist leaders from New England, furious at being dragged into an unwanted war against Great Britain in 1812, threatened secession if the nation did not ratify seven constitutional amendments designed to reduce the power of the South and West (the Republican strongholds) and increase the power of New England. When news of Andrew Jackson's victory at the Battle of New Orleans (1815) arrived in Washington, emissaries from the Hartford Convention were hooted out of town. The public reaction against the Hartford Convention was the fatal blow to the Federalist Party, which now bore the stigma of disloyalty, if not treason. The last Federalist presidential candidate, Rufus King, was obliterated by the Republican James Monroe, 183-34 in the Electoral

College, in 1816. When a second party system arose in the 1830s, the Democrats of Andrew Jackson adopted the pro-agricultural policies of Jefferson's Republican party, and the Whigs of Henry Clay adopted the pro-industrial policies of Hamilton's Federalist party. But, in the antebellum United States' new democratic political culture, the Whigs had neither the inclination nor the ability to adopt the Federalists' aristocratic style and outlook. No aristocratic party could survive an age in which the "common man" was worshiped to such an extent that Daniel Webster considered it necessary to publicly apologize for not having been born in a log cabin, and in which Jackson supporters could campaign against John Quincy Adams with the slogan "Adams can write; Jackson can fight." The death of the Federalist Party represented the death of a formerly powerful American aristocratic tradition never to be reborn and the birth of a new democratic order whose expansion even Jefferson could not have envisioned.

Finally, while the Louisiana Purchase provided the basis for the United States' immense power in the twentieth century, it also helped produce its dissolution in 1861. The acquisition of the new territory led to the first sectional crisis over the question of the expansion of slavery, the issue which was to produce the Civil War. Antebellum white southerners believed they needed new slave territory in order to maintain their power in the Senate, to sustain their standard of living, and to prevent slave insurrections by dispersing the slave population. While most northern whites were willing to turn a blind eye to slavery, since they themselves disfranchised and segregated African-Americans in their own region, they were increasingly determined to keep the territories free. They feared that slavery would drive out free labor in the West. The existence of cheap western land gave northeastern factory workers leverage over their employers. The knowledge that workers possessed the option of obtaining western land forced factory owners to treat them far more fairly than European factory workers were treated (a benefit later lost to massive immigration and the closing of the frontier). Northeastern workers' economic leverage would be lost if the West were monopolized by large planters. There was also an element of racism in some northerners' opposition to the expansion of slavery. When Stephen Douglas accused Abraham Lincoln of advocating interracial marriage, Lincoln replied, "Just because I do not want a black woman for a slave does not mean that I want her for my wife." Knowing his audience well, Lincoln added that it was the slaveholders who mated with black women. To restrict slavery, then, was to restrict contact between the races.

The first crisis occurred in 1819, when Missouri applied to enter the Union as a slave state, thereby threatening the crucial balance between free and slave states, on which rested the balance in the Senate. So great were the passions on both sides that Jefferson wrote from Monticello: "It is the most portentous question which ever threatened our Union. In the gloomiest moment of the revolutionary war I never had any apprehension equal to what I feel from this source. . . . This momentous question, like a fire bell in the night, awakened and filled me with terror. I considered it at once the knell of the Union." Henry Clay's Missouri Compromise (1820) settled the dispute by allowing Maine to enter the Union as a free state, thereby balancing Missouri, and by determining that all Louisiana Purchase Territory south of Thirty-Six Degrees, Thirty Minutes would be slave and all territory north of that line except for Missouri itself would be free. The controversy subsided until California applied for entrance to the Union as a free state in 1849, threatening the balance of fifteen free and fifteen slave states. Clay, now old and tubercular, helped save the day once again with the Compromise of 1850. But Stephen Douglas' Kansas-Nebraska Act (1854) destroyed the delicate framework which held the Union together. The act repealed the Missouri Compromise, allowing the territorial legislatures of Kansas and Nebraska to adopt slavery if they so desired. Northerners felt betrayed. A sacred pact had been violated. The result was the sectionalization of the political parties. The

Democratic Party passed more and more into southern hands, leading to decisions that drove out even more northerners. The act was the final blow to the weak Whig Party. While southern Whigs migrated to the Democratic Party, northern Whigs and Democrats joined together to form the new Republican Party, named after Jefferson's old party. But unlike the Republican Party of Jefferson, the new Republican Party of Lincoln was dedicated to ending the expansion of slavery. Once broad coalitions which served as the principal vehicles for sectional compromise, the political parties had now become the principal organs for sectional warfare. Though possessing absolutely no southern support (the party was not even allowed on the ballot in most southern states), the Republican Party elected Lincoln president with purely northern support in 1860. The results were the secession of the Deep South, the attack on Fort Sumter, and the Civil War. Although a long-term blessing for the United States, the Louisiana Purchase and the further expansionism it encouraged constituted a short-term blight.

Conclusion

Thomas Jefferson once listed the Declaration of Independence, the Virginia Statute of Religious Freedom, and the University of Virginia as the three contributions to American life for which he wished to be remembered. While each of these was a significant contribution, only one, the Declaration of Independence, had a greater impact on American society than the Louisiana Purchase. The Louisiana Purchase was the greatest achievement of the Jefferson Administration—some critics would even say the only real accomplishment in an otherwise bumbling presidency.

SELECTED BIBLIOGRAPHY

The French Colonial Background of Louisiana

Caruso, John A. *The Mississippi Valley Frontier: The Age of French Exploration and Settlement*. Indianapolis: Bobbs-Merill, 1966.

Crouse, Nellis M. *Le Moyne d'Iberville: Soldier of France*. Ithaca: Cornell University Press, 1954.

Eccles, William J. *France in America*. New York: Harper and Row, 1972.

Furneaux, Rupert. *The Seven Years' War*. London: Hart-Davis MacGibbon, 1973.

Gayarré, Charles E. A. *History of Louisiana*. 2d. ed. 4 vols. New York: W. J. Widdleton, 1867.

McDermott, John F., ed. *Frenchmen and French Ways in the Mississippi Valley*. Urbana: University of Illinois Press, 1969.

McWilliams, Richebourg G. *Fleur de Lys and Calumet*. Baton Rouge: Louisiana State University Press, 1953.

Morison, Samuel Eliot. *Samuel de Champlain: Father of New France*. Boston: Little, Brown, and Co., 1972.

Peckham, Howard H. *The Colonial Wars, 1689-1762*. Chicago: University of Chicago Press, 1964.

Early American Expansionism

Alden, John R. *A History of the American Revolution.* New York: Alfred A. Knopf, 1969.

Bemis, Samuel Flagg. *The Diplomacy of the American Revolution.* 2d. ed. Bloomington: Indiana University Press, 1957.

Burns, Edward M. *The American Idea of Mission: Concepts of National Purpose and Destiny.* New Brunswick, N.J.: Rutgers University Press, 1957.

Kaplan, Lawrence S. *From Colonies into Nation: American Diplomacy, 1763-1801.* New York: Macmillan, 1972.

Merk, Frederick. *Manifest Destiny and Mission in American History.* New York, 1963.

Middlekauff, Robert. *The Glorious Cause: The American Revolution, 1763-1789.* Oxford: Oxford University Press, 1982.

Morris, Richard B. *The Peacemakers: The Great Powers and American Independence.* New York: Harper and Row, 1965.

Smith, Henry Nash. *Virgin Land: The American West as Symbol and Myth.* Cambridge, Mass.: Harvard University Press, 1950.

Stourzh, Gerald. *Benjamin Franklin and American Foreign Policy.* Chicago: University of Chicago Press, 1954.

Van Alstyne, Richard W. *The Rising American Empire.* Oxford: Oxford University Press, 1960.

Spanish Louisiana

Brasseaux, Carl A. *"Scattered to the Wind": Dispersals and Wanderings of the Acadians, 1755-1809.* Lafayette: Center forLouisiana Studies, 1991.

McDermott, John F., ed. *The Spanish in the Mississippi Valley, 1762-1804.* Urbana: University of Illinois Press, 1974.

Federalists and Republicans

Bemis, Samuel Flagg. *Pinckney's Treaty: America's Advantage from Europe's Distress, 1783-1800.* New Haven: Yale University Press, 1960.

Bowman, Albert H. *The Struggle for Neutrality: Franco-American Diplomacy during the Federalist Era.* Knoxville: University of Tennessee Press, 1974.

Combs, Jerald A. *The Jay Treaty: Political Background of the Founding Fathers.* Berkeley: University of California Press, 1970.

De Conde, Alexander. *Entangling Alliance: Politics and Diplomacy under George Washington.* Durham, N.C.: Duke University Press, 1958.

---. *The Quasi-War: The Politics and Diplomacy of the Undeclared War with France, 1797-1801.* New York: Scribner, 1966.

Elkins, Stanley and McKitrick, Eric. *The Federalist Era.* Oxford: Oxford University Press, 1993.

Kaplan, Lawrence S. *Jefferson and France: An Essay on Politics and Political Ideas.* New Haven: Yale University Press, 1967.

Kohn, Richard H. *Eagle and Sword: The Federalists and the Creation of the Military Establishment in America, 1783-1802.* New York: Free Press, 1975.

Lycan, Gilbert L. *Alexander Hamilton and American Foreign Policy:A Design for Greatness.* Norman: University of Oklahoma Press, 1970.

Miller, John C. *The Federalist Era, 1789-1801.* New York: Harper and Brothers, 1960.

Stourzh, Gerald. *Alexander Hamilton and the Idea of Republican Government.* Stanford: Stanford University Press, 1970.

Varg, Paul A. *Foreign Policies of the Founding Fathers.* EastLansing: Michigan State University Press, 1963.

The Purchase

Ammon, Harry. *James Monroe: The Quest for National Identity.* New York: McGraw-Hill, 1971.

Bakeless, John E. *The Adventures of Lewis and Clark.* Boston: Houghton-Mifflin, 1962.

Bernard, Jack F. *Talleyrand: A Biography.* New York: Putnam, 1973.

Dangerfield, George. *Chancellor Robert R. Livingston of New York.* New York: Harcourt Brace, 1960.

De Conde, Alexander. *This Affair of Louisiana.* Baton Rouge: Louisiana State University Press, 1976.

Lyon, E. Wilson. *Louisiana in French Diplomacy, 1759-1804.* Norman: University of Oklahoma Press, 1974.

---. *The Man Who Sold Louisiana: The Career of Francois Barbe-Marbois.* Norman: University of Oklahoma Press, 1942.

Kerber, Linda K. *Federalists in Dissent: Imagery and Ideology in Jeffersonian America.* Ithaca: Cornell University Press, 1970.

Korngold, Ralph. *Citizen Toussaint.* Boston: Little, Brown, and Co., 1944.

Ott, Thomas O. *The Haitian Revolution, 1789-1804.* Knoxville: University of Tennessee Press, 1973.

Patterson, Caleb P. *The Constitutional Principles of Thomas Jefferson.* Austin: University of Texas Press, 1953.

Smelser, Marshall. *The Democratic Republic, 1801-1815.* New York: Harper and Row, 1968.

Sprague, Marshall. *So Vast So Beautiful a Land: Louisiana and the Purchase.* Boston: Little, Brown, and Co., 1974.

Whitaker, Arthur. *The Mississippi Question, 1795-1803: A Study in Trade, Politics, and Diplomacy.* New York: D. Appleton-Century Co., 1934.

Wright, J. Leitch, Jr. *Britain and the American Frontier, 1783-1815.* Athens, Ga.: University of Georgia Press, 1975.

Pastoralism

Griswold, A. Whitney. "Jefferson's Agrarian Democracy." In *Thomas Jefferson and American Democracy*. Edited by Henry C. Dethloff. Lexington, Mass.: D.C. Heath, 1971.

McCoy, Drew R. *The Elusive Republic: Political Economy in Jeffersonian America*. Chapel Hill: University of North Carolina Press, 1980.

Richard, Carl J. *The Founders and the Classics: Greece, Rome, and the American Enlightenment*. Cambridge, Mass.: Harvard University Press, 1994.